Emma Hayes Chronicles

Triumphs, Challenges, and the Evolution of Women's Football

Mandate Writers

Content

Introduction

Emma Carol Hayes OBE is an English professional football manager currently managing FA WSL club Chelsea Women. She is set to take over as the manager of the United States women's national team after the 2023–24 season.

Before her current role, Hayes served as the head coach and director of football operations for Chicago Red Stars in the Women's Professional Soccer League in the United States from 2008 to 2010.

She will leave Chelsea at the end of the 2023–24 Women's Super League season to assume her new role with the United States women's national team.

Born in Camden, London, Hayes attended Parliament Hill School and later studied at Liverpool Hope University, graduating in 1999. She initially joined Arsenal's academy but had to end her playing career at 17 due to an ankle injury. Subsequently, Hayes pursued studies in European studies, Spanish, and sociology at Liverpool Hope College. She later earned a master's degree in intelligence and international affairs.

In 2023, Hayes co-authored a book titled "Kill The Unicorn," released in audio format with her as the narrator. The book, more of a leadership manual than a memoir, draws on her high-performance management experience, challenging the perception of a single great leader as a myth.

In 2018, Hayes faced a personal challenge, being pregnant with twins but unfortunately losing one two weeks into the pregnancy. She gave birth to the surviving twin on May 17, 2018.

Hayes acknowledges Vic Akers, the former Arsenal W.F.C. manager, as a significant influence on her career. She was part of the backroom staff under Akers when Arsenal achieved an unprecedented quadruple in the 2006–07 season. Reflecting on her coaching experience in the United States, Hayes expressed that despite being born in England, she feels she was "definitely made in America."

Chelsea forward Fran Kirby, who battled severe depression and a career-threatening illness, has a close relationship with Hayes. Kirby praised Hayes for being her rock and ensuring her protection during challenging times.

Former Chelsea and England player Karen Carney also commended Hayes for being there for her during vulnerable and isolated moments.

Career

Hayes began her coaching career as the manager of the Long Island Lady Riders in 2002, earning recognition as the USL W-League coach of the season.

Subsequently, she assumed the position of head women's soccer coach at Iona College in New Rochelle in January 2003, where she stayed until the conclusion of the 2005 season. Additionally, Hayes served as the first team assistant coach and academy director for Arsenal Ladies from 2006 to 2008.

In May 2008, Hayes took on the role of manager for the Chicago Red Stars. Following her departure in 2010, she transitioned to a technical director role at Western New York Flash, contributing to their success in winning the 2011 Women's Professional Soccer championship.

After consulting for Washington Freedom, Hayes briefly worked for Covent Garden FX, her family's currency exchange business, upon returning to London.

During the mid-season break of the 2012 Summer Olympics, Chelsea appointed Hayes as manager for the remainder of the 2012 season. She managed her first match with Chelsea in August 2012, securing a 1–0 win against Doncaster Rovers Belles.

In the 2022 New Year Honours, Hayes was recognized with the Officer of the Order of the British Empire (OBE) for her contributions to association football.

After narrowly missing the 2014 FA WSL 1 title, Hayes orchestrated a significant squad overhaul, bringing in players like Hedvig Lindahl, Millie Bright, Marija Banusic, Gemma Davison, Niamh Fahey, and Fran Kirby.

Despite initial setbacks, Hayes led Chelsea to a historic league and cup double, winning the FA Cup Final and The FA WSL 1 title in the same season. In the Women's Champions League, Chelsea reached the last 16 but faced criticism from Hayes for fixture scheduling biases favouring certain teams over others.

Hayes's team secured a second-place finish in The FA WSL 1, trailing Champions Manchester City by five points. Despite reaching the FA Cup Final for the second consecutive year and facing a strong Arsenal side, Chelsea suffered a 1–0 defeat. However, they clinched the FA WSL Spring Series, leading the table on goal difference after tying with Manchester City on points.

In the 2016 Birthday Honours, Hayes was appointed a Member of the Order of the British Empire (MBE) for her contributions to football. With the addition of players like Ramona Bachmann, Maren Mjelde, Erin Cuthbert, and

Crystal Dunn, Chelsea finished atop the reorganised FA WSL1 on goal difference. The team reached the FA Cup semi-final but was eliminated by Birmingham City in a penalty shoot-out.

After the 2017–18 season, Hayes undertook a rebuild, bringing in recruits such as Sam Kerr, Pernille Harder, Melanie Leupolz, Magda Eriksson, and Ann Katrin Berger. Chelsea enjoyed back-to-back WSL titles in the 2019–20 and 2020–21 seasons, following a trophy-less 2018–19 campaign.

The team's dominance led to recognition as one of the best, with Hayes becoming the first woman manager to reach the Champions League final in 12 years. However, Chelsea lost 4–0 to Barcelona Femeni in their first-ever Champions League final.

Hayes received the 2020–21 FA WSL Manager of the Season award and signed a new long-term contract with Chelsea. She was inducted into the FA

WSL Hall of Fame and, based on the 2019–20 season, was named The Best FIFA Football Coach on 18 January 2021.

In the 2020–21 season, Hayes secured her third consecutive FA WSL Manager of the Season award, leading Chelsea to the FA Cup and the League domestic double, finishing as runners-up in the League Cup. On 17 January 2022, she was again adjudged The Best FIFA Football Coach for the 2020–21 season.

On 4 November 2023, Chelsea FC announced that Hayes would depart after the ongoing season to pursue a new opportunity outside the WSL and club football. Reports suggested advanced talks for her to become the new manager of the United States women's national team.

On 14 November 2023, Hayes was officially named the Head Coach of the United States women's national team, starting after the WSL season.

Why Hayes is a perfect fit for the US national women's team

In women's football, managing the US national team is considered the biggest job. But is Emma Hayes up to the challenge?

In her 11 years as Chelsea's manager in the Women's Super League, Hayes, 47, has guided the team to 13 major championships, but she feels that the "time is right" to move on.

She will reunite with the four-time world champions after the season, in time for the 2024 Olympic Games, after her much-anticipated move to the United States was finalised on Tuesday.

Hayes has a challenging assignment ahead of her with a new team to lead, a significant tournament approaching, and a great deal of expectation to live up to, but she is more than capable of handling it.

"This is my club and it will always be my club," Hayes declared to the media on Friday, her first public appearance since she announced her resignation from Chelsea.

Although Hayes "hoped it would never come," her decision to end her successful WSL career was ultimately influenced by personal reasons.

Due to her need for family time, especially after her father passed away in October, Hayes decided to pursue international management instead of club football because it offered her more freedom. Hayes is a mother to a five-year-old son named Harry.

"This is a selfless decision, not a selfish one. It involves prioritising other aspects of my life, and I'm prepared for that," Hayes remarked.

Hayes expressed her desire to "leave at the top" and she has accomplished that goal, winning the WSL title for the fourth time in a row last season.

Many coaches aspire to work in the United States because they have an abundance of resources, a stellar track record of accomplishment, and world-class athletes wearing the uniform.

Hayes has previously expressed her wish to lead her nation at important competitions and on the grandest platform.

She was once acknowledged as being "definitely made in America" despite being born in England, and she has experience working in the US as head coach of the Chicago Red Stars.

"As a little girl I always thought maybe one day [managing a national team] would come," Hayes stated last week. "For most of us, we don't necessarily fulfil every dream we have."

Hayes's great significance to US Soccer is another important consideration. She will become the highest-paid female manager in the world thanks to the federation, and she will likely receive the same salary as USA men's captain Gregg Berhalter.

Ellen White, a former England striker, stated: "Her contributions to the game have been incredible. Her advocacy for players and the amazing things she has done for Chelsea, women in sports, and moms in sports are truly remarkable.

"Players just spoke so highly of her, and as the opponent, we always had so much respect for what she's done. Although it will be unfortunate for the WSL, you want to wish her well and hope that her next position is even more fantastic.

"It will undoubtedly be difficult to replace her. But we're appreciative of what she accomplished here. She may not have done so against some of the teams I was playing for, but her contributions to the game are incredible."

Another former Lioness, Jill Scott, stated: "She's finished WSL, isn't that right? It will be tough on whoever walks into Chelsea now. It bears similarities to Alex Ferguson's departure from Manchester United."

Every football management position has some level of strain. However, nothing comes close to the weight of expectations put on the president of the United States of America.

They are the most decorated country in the history of women's football, having won four times, including two consecutive titles in 2015 and 2019.

In addition, they have won four gold medals at the Olympics. The United States has held the top spot in the Fifa rankings for a total of thirteen years since the rankings were introduced in 2003.

However, this is a transitional USA squad.

Just three months have passed since their shocking last-16 loss at the Women's World Cup, their lowest-ever result in the competition that precipitated their first-ever drop to third in the world rankings.

Prominent players who contributed to the United States' remarkable triumph have retired from the game, including Julie Ertz, a pivotal midfielder, and Megan Rapinoe, a legendary goal scorer.

Hayes will need to develop a fresh crop of talent that is emerging. Even though she has access to talented people like Naomi Girma, 23, Sophia Smith, 23, and Trinity Rodman, 21, it's still a challenging project.

Fans in the United States will not accept anything less than gold at the Olympics in Paris, and Hayes won't have much time to get her team ready for a major international competition.

Hayes thrives under pressure, despite the obstacles.

She had to defeat advancing opponents every season after leading Chelsea to the top of the WSL.

In addition to winning five Women's FA Cups, two Women's League Cups, and leading Chelsea to their first-ever Women's Champions League final in 2021, she has been able to accomplish this effectively for four seasons in a row.

She carried on challenging federations on issues like equitable prize money and scheduling competitions while doing this.

"I know my personality and I'm not afraid to do the tough things even though sometimes I'm the one who takes the battering from it," Hayes remarked.

According to US Soccer, the candidate is a perfect fit for the position because of her background in the country, familiarity with the soccer scene here, and understanding of what it takes to coach this team.

"Candidates underwent an intense and thorough interview process which included psychometrics and abstract reasoning tests, in-depth discussions of strategy, coaching philosophy and the current player pool, as well as evaluation on the reactions to pressure, culture-building and interactions with players and staff."

During her tenure at Chelsea, Hayes has also seen some key players depart, but she has been able to assemble a strong squad by hiring qualified replacements during the transfer window, proving her capacity for continuous improvement.

Playmaker Ji So-yun's departure in 2022 was mitigated by the signing of Serb Jelena Jankovic and five-time Champions League winner Kadeisha Buchanan. Meanwhile, the departures of captain Magdalena Eriksson and striker Pernille Harder, for whom Chelsea once paid a world record fee, this summer were offset by the signings of Canadian Ashley Lawrence and USA internationals Mia Fishel and Catarina Macario.

Finding creative ways to maintain her position of success is one of Hayes's other strong points.

She has authored a book on leadership, enlisted the help of sleep specialists, consulted US basketball coaches, and regularly brought scientists and physicians into Chelsea to impart their expertise on training loads and menstrual cycles.

Scott stated: "Every single player that I talk to who has played under Emma just says that her emotional intelligence and how she gets the best out of the players is on another level."

Chelsea player Anita Asante, who was coached by Hayes, stated: "She's always supported me no matter what throughout my career." When things became tough or I was at the bottom of my football career, she was that one reliable person I knew I could always count on.

"I never had any doubts that she would be there to assist me at this difficult time, even when I picked up the phone.

"She would counsel me or assist me in determining the best course of action. That, in my opinion, illustrates how she values each player as an individual first. That's significant, in my opinion, and the reason our friendship has lasted this long."

Hayes has all the qualities that make him an excellent contender, but the USA is most in need of a manager who knows how to win, and Hayes has demonstrated this ability time and time again.

Emma Hayes' most significant WSL games

Emma Hayes has had an incredibly successful managing career at Chelsea, but when the Women's Super League season ends in May, her tenure there will come to an end.

In her career with the team, Hayes has won 13 major titles. She also helped Chelsea reach the Women's Champions League final for the first time.

Throughout her 11-year career, there have been many memorable games; BBC Sport chooses five of the best and analyses their effects.

1. 2015: Chelsea 1-0 Notts County
Usually, the sweetest prize is the first one. Hayes signed with Chelsea in 2012, but it took some time for the team to recover before she took home her first trophy.

When Ji So-Yun, one of her most successful acquisitions, scored the game-winning goal in the 2015 FA Cup final against Notts County, it finally arrived in 2015.

It was the first Women's FA Cup to be hosted at Wembley Stadium, and it was special to Hayes as her maiden prize as well as Chelsea's first piece of silverware.

Chelsea entered the championship game having lost their last two league games, but as we have seen, under Hayes, they rarely lose when there are trophies on the line.

2. 2021: Bayern Munich 1-4 Chelsea (agg 5-3)

Although Hayes experienced some moments of success in her career, winning games became increasingly difficult as her Chelsea dynasty grew.

Chelsea still has yet to win a Women's Champions League championship, but Hayes guided the team to its first-ever final in 2021 when they thrillingly defeated Bayern Munich in the semifinals.

Superstars Pernille Harder and Fran Kirby scored goals late in the second leg to help Chelsea, behind 2-1 after the first leg, triumph 4-1 at home and go to the final.

The win over Bayern Munich cnsured that an English team challenged for the title for the first time in 14 years, and Hayes broke down in tears after the final whistle. They would go on to lose badly, 4-0, to Barcelona.

3. 2022: Chelsea 3-0 Tottenham

Chelsea and Tottenham, who live nearby in London, have played several important games, including the latter's inaugural WSL match at Stamford Bridge in 2019.

However, Hayes found great significance in this game as it was her first since her return from an emergency hysterectomy, and the triumph ultimately contributed to her fourth consecutive WSL crown.

After nearly two months apart, Hayes described returning on the pitch as "like being back with family" as Chelsea won 3-0 with goals from Sam Kerr, Erin Cuthbert, and Guro Reiten.

Additionally, a record-breaking 38,300 spectators watched the game at Stamford Bridge, home of Chelsea women.

4. 2023: Chelsea 1-2 Lyon (agg 2-2)

Hayes holds a special place in her heart for the Women's Champions League, which is also the prize she has wanted most during her time there.

Although Chelsea's unwavering pursuit of European success has produced some unforgettable moments, their quarterfinal triumph over the defending champions Lyon ranks among Chelsea's best-ever performances.

After an incredible two-leg match that culminated in a thrilling penalty shootout, Chelsea custodian Ann-Katrin Berger made two vital stops to keep Lindsey Horan and Wendie Renard out of the game.

The fact that it took place at Stamford Bridge and that Chelsea was given a penalty in the last seconds of extra time thanks in part to the technology employed by the video assistant referee (VAR) was another example of how far the women's game has progressed during Hayes' tenure at the club.

Eight-time champions Lyon lost in the quarterfinals for just the second time in their last 14 quarter final appearances, and Chelsea's triumph ensured that, for the first time in five years, there were two

English teams in the final four when they joined Arsenal in the semifinals.

5. 2023: Chelsea 3–0 Reading

The benefits received subsequently made this match noteworthy.

Chelsea secured their fourth consecutive WSL title with a victory over Reading on the last day of the previous campaign, sending the home team into relegation in the process.

It is an incredible accomplishment to win four league titles in a row, and Hayes seemed more thoughtful than normal as she took in what her players and staff had accomplished.

The victory ended after a season in which Hayes had surgery, had to contend with maintaining a demanding work-life balance while taking care of her infant son Harry, and had to overcome obstacles presented by stronger opponents. Hayes called it "the hardest one yet."

On the pitch, she was overcome with emotion as she and Harry celebrated Chelsea's victory, posed for pictures with her son and the trophy in front of fans, and bid farewell to striker Harder and key club captain Magdalena Eriksson.

This was maybe Hayes' most satisfying trophy to date, but before she departs Chelsea in the summer, she will hopefully have one more title triumph.

How Emma Hayes changed WSL forever

When Emma Hayes departs Chelsea at the end of the current campaign, she will go down in history as one of the club's finest managers; her contribution to the expansion of the Women's Super League should also not be overlooked.

Hayes has led the Blues since 2012, and Chelsea revealed on Saturday that he will leave in the summer to explore "a new opportunity outside the WSL and club football".

Her tenure has been nothing short of extraordinary; between 2019 and 2023, she won four consecutive WSL titles, among 13 other significant prizes.

Hayes, who is widely seen as one of the most important coaches in the game, created the Chelsea dynasty that has allowed them to rule English football for the last ten years.

In addition to completely changing Chelsea, the 47-year-old also set the groundwork for the team's future success.

Hayes brought with her the knowledge and training she had acquired while working for the Chicago Red Stars as head coach and director of football operations while she was in the United States when she initially joined the team in 2012. After leaving Chelsea, she's a strong contender to take over as manager of the US national team, so she may head back home.

Hayes first witnessed the potential of women's football in the USA, where the sport was leading internationally. She dreamed of the day when English football would catch up to this level of play.

Hayes set out to assemble a team that could provide her with the leverage she needed to negotiate for what she wanted, knowing that success on the pitch would assist her with the means to do so.

Chelsea provided Hayes and her team with off-field assistance as they excelled on the pitch. The West London club and its manager, who was born in Camden, have together set the bar that his WSL competitors are now trying to meet.

Although Hayes's 11-year term and numerous awards have catapulted her into the public eye, her impact at Chelsea will extend well beyond the boundaries of the football pitch where she teaches.

Using science and research to explore areas that had not previously been examined, Hayes explored every path for success during her WSL career, pushing the league, her team, and her staff to continually improve.

As an advocate for women's health, she has pushed for education on nutrition, supported studies on the connections between female football players and anterior cruciate ligament (ACL) injuries, and promoted studies on menstrual cycle patterns.

Hayes has made sure Chelsea is constantly ahead of the pack and has adjusted alongside the league, even as the women's game in England has continued to change on the pitch.

During Hayes' rule, Manchester United, Arsenal, and City have all presented challenges, but it is impossible to overestimate her capacity to keep a winning culture and bolster the team every transfer window.

Her players had all they needed to perform in a professional setting, and Hayes eliminated every reason why they couldn't win.

Her brutality, which has brought her great success, was demonstrated in the club's 2022 DAZN documentary. In one video, she gave a team speech during which she threatened to "find better ones" in place of her players if they failed to perform.

Throughout her Chelsea tenure, Hayes has found success with this strategy, specifically selecting individuals in the transfer market who she knew would flourish in a difficult setting.

Despite opposition from six-time European champions Lyon, Hayes pulled off one of her greatest coups in 2018 when she signed Australia striker Sam Kerr, following their elimination from the Women's Champions League semi-finals.

A year later, as Hayes went after that elusive European title, Chelsea paid a world record amount to recruit Pernille Harder of Wolfsburg.

Even though Hayes has only missed out on one trophy in her Chelsea career, her team has made more progress towards winning it than any other English team since Arsenal's historic victory in

2007—a year in which Hayes was the assistant manager for the Gunners.

What will be most applauded when Hayes departs in the summer as Chelsea's most decorated head coach is how many trophies she has won.

The influence she has had on the future of the English women's game, however, is her greatest legacy.

Hayes has had a huge impact on the development of the game as a motivator of professional standards in the WSL, a role model for female coaches, and an advocate for equal chances.

Despite the huge void her departure would leave at Chelsea, she has established systems to support recruitment, scientific research, and youth development.

She has established expectations for achievement on the field, given female coaches the strength to confront preconceptions, and inspired her players to assume leadership roles and grow into responsible individuals.

Regardless of the everyday imprint Hayes leaves, women's football in England will never be the same. She is the reason it will be better.

The Secrets of Emma Hayes' title successes at Chelsea

When pressed to share the keys of Chelsea's success, manager Emma Hayes remained reticent.

In the season's last game, a 3-0 victory over Reading guaranteed a fourth Women's Super League title in a row. With the win, Hayes achieved a league and FA Cup double, her 14th major title since joining the team in 2012.

Despite increased funding and rivalry from its rivals, Chelsea continues to rule English women's football.

"Do you think I'm going to give away the crown jewels?" Earlier last month, Hayes made a joke on Sky Sports.

"These are the secrets to our success, so I'm not going to spill it on national TV."

Hayes' strategy of keeping things close to the vest is understandable given that whatever it is, it is effective.

Chelsea constantly fights for every honour; this year, they lost in the League Cup final and advanced to the semifinals of the Champions League.

Following the squad's triumph over championship rivals Arsenal last weekend, Hayes remarked, "I know the work that has gone on behind the scenes to get the team to where it is."

"All I notice when I look at the pitch is the years of labour that have been done in the backdrop. The conversations, the debates, the meetings, the enjoyable times, and the times when you're tired of staring at each other.

"It's all of those things, and when they come off this team has a habit of peaking when it matters." Observation of detail

Chelsea's most notable asset under Hayes may be their consistent performance throughout crucial moments of the season.

Chelsea steps it up as the effects of a demanding schedule start to show in the teams around them.

Claire Rafferty, a former Blues defender who was Hayes' teammate from 2012 to 2016, stated that the "commitment to small details," including having a variety of specialists on her backroom staff, gave them an advantage over their competitors.

Rafferty said to BBC Sport, "There were more staff than players at one point."

"It involved making sure the girls had the appropriate mattresses to sleep on and bringing in a sleep coach to supplement the physiotherapist, medical personnel, and massage therapist.

"We looked at hormone supplements when you were on your period and monitored training loads after we had one-on-one dietary assistance.

"What impressed me was Hayes' willingness to admit when she wasn't an authority on a subject. For her to concentrate on overseeing the players, we even had someone step in to virtually lead the other personnel."

"It started slowly, but it's picked up speed."

It took some time to grasp how these adjustments would affect Chelsea's success.

Rafferty admits that at the time, she considered some of it laborious. "We had to do something else and sit in another meeting," she explained.

It was unfamiliar to us. When I think back on it, we were maybe a touch too ungrateful at the time—something I hate to admit.

"You only wanted to play football because you lived in a bubble. People now recognise that the game is more than simply what happens on the pitch and value it as a complete. It's how you prepare your body, and safeguard both your physical and mental health."

The players' perspective shifted as Chelsea began to succeed. It was now an essential ritual rather than a hassle. It was acknowledged that achieving trophy success necessitated a daily, motivated culture.

"I think Emma was probably always aware [of what impact it would have]," Rafferty added.

"She would enter many clubs across the globe and observe their activities. She would take advice from people. The amount of money and effort required to get there meant that the process had to be gradual.

"'If you're winning, I can ask for more money,' she would always say. It's vivid in my memory. "You need to win so I can feed you and have a leg to stand on," she would remark.

"It started slowly, but it picked up speed. We started to succeed in 2015, which is when we first started to take it seriously."

"That team is unsafe for anyone." At Chelsea, winning trophies is now expected.

Their incessant hoarding of domestic trophies makes it nearly impossible to imagine them not winning anything throughout a season.

So how has Chelsea managed to keep up their trophy chase and repel stronger opponents?

"You can't stay motionless as Chelsea's rivalry intensifies. You bring in players that have a newfound will to succeed "Rafferty stated.

"You have to keep a squad young; you don't get tired of winning. Players who don't settle for second best have been drawn to Hayes."

When Chelsea signed Danish forward Pernille Harder in 2020, they smashed the global transfer record. Lauren James, the teenage sensation from Manchester United, was signed by them a year later.

They signed Lyon's five-time Champions League victor Kadeisha Buchanan last year.

Hayes has been able to rotate well and frequently in four tournaments this season because of the addition of quality and the bolstering of Chelsea's roster depth.

"In that squad, nobody is safe. You have to put up a struggle to go in there and do it. Rafferty stated that training is a major platform for such.

"The climate fosters that mentality, which is why I recall being so sad when we lost in training. Competition is constant.

"Hayes is interested in more than just the player on the field; he is interested in how that player handles pressure and responds to missing four games in a row due to an opponent's performance.

"It's the players' mindset—they never settle down." They sense that someone is pursuing them, so they are constantly checking over their shoulders."

Hayes' hidden trauma, ADHD and Chelsea's upheaval

Amid the uncertainty, Hayes is content in his modest Cobham bungalow as a new era emerges at Chelsea's closely watched training facility. The owners of Chelsea fired Thomas Tuchel two weeks ago, the morning after his 100th game with the team, just a short stroll away.

Hayes had just completed a decade leading Chelsea Women, a tenure distinguished by five Women's Super League championships, four FA Cups, and two League Cups.

Her son Harry was born just thirty minutes before Hayes gave birth to his twin brother Albie, who had passed away within twenty-eight weeks, and this coincided with the second half of her tenure at Chelsea. She seemed to have been freed from four years of trauma that was concealed.

The affable and candid Hayes has shared her thoughts on her loss and grief while also expressing sympathy for Tuchel. The 45-year-old has discussed her diagnosis of ADHD in the past and recalled being pushed to "change the face of women's football" by her father.

Before announcing her "dream job" in football and speaking fluent Spanish, Hayes made suggestions about how to effectively capitalise on England's victory at Euro 2022.

On a bright afternoon, Hayes shares these intriguing thoughts as she beams with vitality and says, "I had an off-season taking in life and enjoying anything from a walk to a drink." Not surprisingly, I feel the freshest I've ever felt. I always manage to read, learn, and maintain my interest. However, life was my study this summer.

In my career, I've also arrived at a place where I'm truly enjoying it. Years went by when I didn't, but these days I adore the work. I've been working on a football model my entire career, and it's coming together. The team has a wonderful energy and all the jigsaw pieces fit together well, so it's obvious that we'll continue to compete.

As the new season gets underway, Hayes—the greatest manager in the WSL—hopes to lead Chelsea to a fourth straight championship. "I've recovered," she declares. "After being wrong for the last four years, I feel better than I have since before I gave birth." I hadn't considered that I still needed to deliver two babies when I realised I would only be able to deliver one live child.

All I had to do was bring Harry into the world in good health. However, I now understand why women take a year off work following childbirth: I was unprepared for the substantial hormonal, physical, and psychological strain.

"My return to work after eight weeks was my biggest regret." It has nothing to do with the team because how do you take a year off from managing football players?

What happens if they hire a temporary coach and decide to continue with him or her after eight months? The club would have offered me their full support, but I felt like I was in an impossible situation.

Hayes remembers the emptiness of losing Albie, and her face shows her wounds. "I will always be in that moment, and I feel bad for Harry since he doesn't have a brother. Though I accept it, I can't claim it doesn't hurt right now.

I will continue to grieve about it on Christmas and my birthday. That is typical. But I was just trying to get by throughout those first four years. I felt worn out. But this May, when Harry turned four, I woke up. That was the first moment I realised I was back. I'm back.

She has returned to the chaos of football, which is exemplified by Chelsea's men's squad. In the years since Hayes joined in 2012, bringing structure and stability, there have been ten male managers, including carers. After 20 months in which Chelsea won the Champions League, Tuchel's dismissal was the most recent development in the managerial turmoil.

Hayes tells me, "I'm gutted," just before Graham Potter took Tuchel's job. "I cherish Thomas. He is a wonderful man and coach who has experienced a tremendous deal of change over his brief career.

Though it disappoints me and makes me very sad for him, Thomas will succeed anywhere. Did she and Tuchel discuss football in depth? Indeed, we managed to find time, but it's short-lived when you can spare an hour for it. We got along pretty well together.

Hayes emphasises how much she has missed working with the previous administration, particularly Bruce Buck, the former chairman. "For me, Bruce has been enormous. He is already missed.

He's a fantastic Chelsea man who encouraged me to keep pushing the club because, as an American, he truly understood the women's game. I was devastated when he and Marina Granovskaia, the former director who oversaw contracts and transfers, left since I always felt so trusted by them.

"There's always anxiety when there's change. However, Bruce stated: "It's going to be different but that doesn't mean it's going to be worse" during the takeover [when Roman Abramovich sold Chelsea to a group led by the American billionaire Todd Boehly]. "I want you to be open to change," is something I tell my players all the time. That was something I had to undertake on my own.

Has she talked to Boehly much? Yes, I do talk to Todd regularly. I believe our current ownership group will be the champions of women's football based on my contacts with them. They can elevate women's football in this nation, which makes me very happy.

As a coach, Hayes has been so impressive that some Chelsea supporters and commentators, like Pat Nevin, have argued Boehly ought to have given her some thought as a possible Tuchel replacement.

Although Hayes is devoted to Chelsea Women and often detests being questioned about leading a men's team, it's interesting to note her response when I ask her about her biggest frustration.

"The Sky Sports headline which suggested I said it was an insult to coach AFC Wimbledon. That was my biggest pet peeve. Since then, I've informed Sky of how extremely risky it is to make such a declaration. I didn't claim that the AFC Wimbledon coach was being insulted.

I answered, "Coaching these women is not an insult," referring to my athletes. Nothing, not even money, could separate me from honouring the women I represented.

"Chelsea Women received a critical letter from the chairman of AFC Wimbledon. He made a grave error of judgement because we use their stadium. I answer that question regarding the men's game all the time, but it was distressing when Sky Sports published a headline that would seriously harm any woman in that circumstance.

Although Sky's coverage of the women's game has changed, I am aware that everything I say will only serve as clickbait.

Simon Jordan once stated that women aren't equipped to coach male athletes since they aren't accustomed to doing it in front of big crowds. Hayes shrugs this comment off. It struck me as the most absurd thing I had ever heard.

Jordan's argument was completely refuted by the summer's European Championships, which were frequently held in front of enormous, crowded stadiums as female coaches and athletes demonstrated bravery, skill, tactical awareness, and technical genius.

However, Hayes feels that women's football needs to break away from the Football Association to grow after the Euro boom. She anticipates that the Premier League will have recognised the benefits of holding a competition of a similar nature for women.

"If they or another independent body doesn't show real interest, I'd be startled. Due to their experience managing a league with a significant international influence, I favour the Premier League. We need to take advantage of the fact that everyone is focusing on England. It will take us longer to accomplish our goals the longer we are under the FA's control."

Hayes has been driven to speak up ever since her father gave her the directive to spearhead the change in women's football. "As a father of three living in the heart of Camden Town in the mid-1990s, he told one of his daughters, 'It's up to me to transform the face of women's football.

At the age of 20, I completed my B licence in coaching and had a very snobbish experience. "You have to go to America," he declared. You must leave this place. Return when you're prepared to alter the story.

He insisted that it was my responsibility to raise the issue, saying, "You have to talk about the administrators and officials. The professional expectations and standards must be established by you. As a woman, however, speaking up makes you "outspoken, difficult, prickly." I had to endure a little abuse.

Hayes grinned. "I've always been appreciative of my parents' freedom and trust in me. They were aware of my poor performance under duress, and I've always believed that my greatest obstacle would have come from working for the FA. That would have been too much for me to handle; at Chelsea, there was pressure and freedom. Pressure has always been fun for me.

She pauses in contemplation. "I have a different side to myself, and playing football has helped me manage my ADHD. Being a football manager and having to oversee numerous tasks, in my opinion, keeps my brain in excellent shape.

Has she got ADHD? "Chelsea's performance coach is certain that I do. Although I've never received a diagnosis, it all makes perfect sense to me. Throughout my career, however, I have surrounded myself with people who can support me when I am unable to. I'm a huge recluse.

All I want to do when I leave [the training ground] is go home and be by myself, quietly. It's who I've always been. Additionally, I need peace when I leave my job because it requires extroverted behaviour and I spend so much energy here.

Has she changed as a boss since having a mother? 100% of the time. In addition to being incredibly sensitive, my son possesses incredible emotional intelligence. Knowing my kid and vice versa has made me a much better manager of players.

I've become more adept at handling particular players as a result of my education about them and how to control them. How do you handle those that are different from you? or those that you find difficult to understand? This is one of my main areas of interest and fascination.

Would Hayes be happy to coach England in the future? As a club manager and supporter of England, I've loved seeing them both, and as I get older, I believe it's best to never say never about any of these careers. However, coaching in Spain has always been my dream job.

For the next fifteen seconds, she speaks in Spanish. "I have a degree in Spanish and speak the language fluently. Thus, coaching in Spain has always been my ideal profession. Tutoring the English? Don't ever say never.

Hayes smiles again, full of such insights and shocks. Did I anticipate spending ten years at Chelsea? Nope. I wouldn't be shocked if I lived here for an additional ten years. I sincerely enjoy what I do. I am incredibly thankful. I am fortunate. "How have I managed to forge a career in the world that I love most?" is how I feel.

Bonus: The History of women's football

The Women's World Cup final between England and Spain will be seen by millions of viewers.

More than 1.7 million tickets have been sold for the competition in Australia and New Zealand, which is the most well-known women's football match to date.

It represents the most recent pinnacle of interest in women's football, which has been steadily increasing over the past few years despite being overlooked for decades by men's football.

However, things weren't always this way; at one point, the sport was very popular in England.

Huge crowds, often exceeding 50,000 people, were drawn to matches.

However, the FA at the time declared that women's football was "quite unsuitable for females," thus outlawing the sport.

Women's football lagged behind the men's game in part because it took another fifty years for the sport to recover.

One of the first female professional players was the winger Lily Parr.

She was a member of the Dick, Kerr's Ladies team, so named because the majority of the team was employed at the Preston armaments factory during World War One.

They went on an international tour and were the first women's team to play in shorts.

Lily also smoked, which gave rise to claims that she received extra money in the form of Woodbine cigarette packages.

She was the first female football player to be honoured with a statue and the first woman to be admitted into the National Football Museum Hall of Fame in 2002.

Attendance at women's matches was astronomical.

During the war, women were called upon to fill factory jobs vacated by the males who had gone to fight, which led to a great rise in women's football.

Ten thousand people watched two women's teams play at Preston on Christmas Day in 1917.

Additionally, Dick Kerr's Ladies drew a crowd of 53,000 spectators to Everton's Goodison Park field on Boxing Day 1920 when they played St Helen's Ladies, with thousands more fans imprisoned outside.

However, the women's game was essentially outlawed.

The Football Association forbade women from participating in FA-affiliated fields on December 5, 1921, meaning that celebrities like Lily Parr could no longer play in venues with seating for spectators.

"The game of football is quite unsuitable for females and ought not to be encouraged," the FA declared at the time.

Following the founding of the Women's Football Association (WFA) a few years prior, the ban was eventually repealed in 1971.

Fifty years later, women may finally pursue football as a career. Training to become a professional referee was made easier for women by the Sex Discrimination Act of 1975.

Since the 1970s, when the first TV reports of the Women's FA Cup final results were made, watching women's football on television has always been somewhat difficult.

Women's football began to be regularly covered by Channel 4 in 1989.

Additionally, in 1997, the FA announced its plans to advance women's football from amateur to elite status.

The Women's Super League (WSL) didn't fully transition to a professional league until 2018.

According to recent statistics, 3.4 million women and girls in England participate in football.

At Wembley, a record crowd of 87,192 watched England defeat Germany in the Euro 2022 final, marking their first major women's championship victory.

Since then, investments have increased, which has resulted in women receiving higher pay and longer contracts.

With a peak audience of 7.3 million, England's World Cup semi-final matchup against Australia was the most watched of the tournament thus far among UK viewers.

Bonus: Things that held women back in football

A former star player attacked Premier League football clubs for declining the chance to host games during the European Championship they had recently won, just after England's Lionesses achieved history on Sunday.

Alex Scott remarked, "You weren't brave enough to see the vision," in front of a record 87,192 spectators at Wembley during England's 2-1 victory against Germany in the championship match.

Even more people watched it at home, with 17.4 million viewers on BBC One making it the most-watched programme of the year thus far.

English football is currently the subject of a lot of attention as many try to figure out how to profit from a squad that has won the hearts of the country.

But first, what has kept women's and girls' football back for so long? From a lack of educational possibilities to persistent financial constraints, let's talk about these issues.

The FA's 50-year suspension

The Association Football Association (FA), which oversees association football in England, banned women from participating in the sport at any of its associated venues in 1921 because it was deemed "unsuitable for females".

Because officials lacked the authority to overtly forbid women from playing, the FA asked clubs "belonging to the Association [to] refuse the use of their grounds for such matches" in its verdict.

Women's football was quite popular at the time; the trend began during World War One when most males who could play the game were needed for the war effort. Women's football matches satisfied the nation's urge to watch football while it was still being played.

A Boxing Day encounter between Dick's team, Kerr Ladies FC from Preston, and St Helen's Ladies was witnessed by 53,000 people at Goodison Park in Liverpool, which is still home to Everton, just one year before the ban was put in place. 14,000 more people were stuck outside the stadium attempting to enter.

Fifty years later, in 1971, the ban was finally removed, but the harm had already been done. "The interest naturally waned without the opportunity for the masses to watch games regularly in large-capacity venues," says A Woman's Game author Suzy Wrack.

The Women's Super League (WSL) began as a fully professional league just four years ago. With 9,251 teams connected to the FA, 3.4 million women and girls play football in England, according to the most recent statistics.

Given the success of the Lionesses, this number is anticipated to rise. In March, the government announced plans to invest £230 million in grassroots football and unveiled its next phase of pitches and facilities for women.

Girls' football is not offered in schools

Ensuring that every girl in primary school has equal access to football as boys at school and in clubs by 2024 is a major goal of the Football Association's four-year Inspiring Positive Change initiative.

According to their plan, the FA wants to make sure that as many young girls as possible "carry on playing football into and through their teenage years" by funding after-school programmes and collaborating with "grassroots clubs and community football providers".

This year, the association revealed that 63% of English schools offer girls' football in physical education classes, and even fewer—40%—give females regular after-school football. 72% of elementary schools provide the sport; however, as students go into larger year groups, just 44% of schools do so.

One of the BBC's top football commentators, Ian Wright, a former England player, questioned: "Whatever happens in the final now, if girls are not allowed to play football just like the boys can in their PE lessons after this tournament, then what are we doing?" after the Lionesses' 4-0 victory over Sweden in the Euro semi-final last week.

Misogynistic views regarding female athletes

It is common for female football players to experience misogynistic and sexist taunts because of their occupation, and this was evident during the Euros.

According to a study done by the broadsheet Süddeutsche Zeitung, German broadcasters ARD and NDR, and Uefa, out of 300 abusive social media posts found during the contest's group stages:

To combat misogyny in the game, male members of the England team have now teamed up with the Lionesses.

Aiming to combat online sexist hate, EE Hope United, a campaign that revolves around a dream team of football players to end social media abuse, announced a new squad consisting of some of the most well-known male and female players in the UK in the lead-up to the Euros.

TV commercials that aired during the tournament month featured the faces of several celebrities, including Liverpool captain Jordan Henderson, England men's team manager Gareth Southgate,

Lionesses stars Ellen White and Lucy Bronze, and others.

Less funding for sports for women

The elite Women's Super League (WSL) of England was established over a decade ago, but the major money has only recently begun to flow into the women's game. This is because of sponsors, which include companies like Barclays, Visa, and Nike, in addition to more attention in the general public media.

Nonetheless, women's football in England continues to get significantly less funding than men's.

Former England player Alex Scott now says she thinks sponsors will have to show the Lionesses how valuable they are, not the other way around.

"You know what, I'm not going to beg sponsors to support the women's game anymore while I'm speaking at business gatherings. You've missed the train and the boat if you're not participating.

Financial obstacles that girls must overcome to advance

During the Euros, the phrase "pay to play" gained popularity after rumours circulated that parents of females could have to pay for their daughters' access to play at Premier League football clubs, while boys could practise for free at the clubs' academies.

Following an Inews investigation outlining the payments, Gary Lineker has asked the Premier League to do away with the levies, telling teams they need to "sort this out".

The fact that several major clubs have moved their training facilities for young boys and girls from cities into suburbs in recent years has also made the matter worse by making it more difficult for the kids to get to the training grounds.

There is less motivation for parents of young girls to sacrifice other responsibilities to push their sons to the limit and give them the best shot at winning, but parents of boys with the potential to make millions from the sport would.

Fans and athletes alike are optimistic that the way people perceive the women's game will change permanently as the sport continues to gain unprecedented momentum.

Following the success of the Lionesses, the FA has already stated that it wants to see 120,000 more girls play football. Over the next 18 months, the FA will be implementing measures to increase grassroots football and inclusiveness.

I have a request

Dear Reader,

I hope you found "Emma Hayes Chronicles: Triumphs, Challenges, and the Evolution of Women's Football" informative and helpful. I value your opinion and would greatly appreciate it if you could take a moment to share your feedback.

Your review can make a significant difference in helping others make informed decisions about this book. Whether you found the content engaging or the information well-presented, your insight can inspire and guide fellow readers.

If you could spare a few minutes, I would be grateful if you could write a review on platforms such as Goodreads, Amazon, or any other book review website. Your honest feedback will not only assist us in improving our work but also enable us to continue creating valuable resources for readers like you.

Thank you for being part of our journey, and we look forward to hearing your thoughts on "Book title". Your support is immensely appreciated!.

Additional Resources

Thank you for your support and interest in "Emma Hayes Chronicles: Triumphs, Challenges, and the Evolution of Women's Football". If you enjoy this book and are looking for more valuable resources and engaging content, I would like to recommend some of my other books and series that you might find interesting.

To explore these books, please visit my Author central page on Amazon. There, you will find a complete collection of my work, including additional series and resources that may pique your interest. **You can scan the QR code below or click the link to visit my Author Central Page.**

My Author Central page

Printed in Great Britain
by Amazon

34787967R00046